HOW DOES IT WORK?

How Does a HELICOPTER Work?

BY SARAH EASON

Gareth Stevens
Publishing

Please visit our Web site www.garethstevens.com. For a free color catalog of all our high-quality books, call toll free 1-800-542-2595 or fax 1-877-542-2596.

Library of Congress Cataloging-in-Publication Data
Eason, Sarah.
      How does a helicopter work? / Sarah Eason.
         p. cm. — (How does it work?)
      Includes bibliographical references and index.
      ISBN 978-1-4339-3465-0 (library binding)
      ISBN 978-1-4339-3466-7 (pbk.)
      ISBN 978-1-4339-3467-4 (6-pack)
      1. Helicopters—Juvenile literature. I. Title.
   TL716.2.E26 2010
   629.133'352—dc22   2009039326

Published in 2010 by
Gareth Stevens Publishing
111 East 14th Street, Suite 349
New York, NY 10003

© 2010 The Brown Reference Group Ltd.

For Gareth Stevens Publishing:
Art Direction: Haley Harasymiw
Editorial Direction: Kerri O'Donnell

For The Brown Reference Group Ltd:
Editorial Director: Lindsey Lowe
Managing Editor: Tim Harris
Editor: Sarah Eason
Children's Publisher: Anne O'Daly
Design Manager: David Poole
Designer: Paul Myerscough
Production Director: Alastair Gourlay

Picture Credits:
Front cover: Shutterstock: Ungor (background); Brown Reference Group (foreground)

Illustrations by Roger Courthold and Mark Walker

Picture Credits Key: t – top, b – below, c – center, l – left, r – right. Patrick Allen 26; Dreamstime: Monkeybusiness 17; Genesis Space Photo Library 28; GKN?Westland 12; Shutterstock: 6, Anbk 14, Ramon Berk 25, Centrill Media 18-19, Alexandr Kano~kin 8, Charles F McCarthy 27,   Steve Rosset 20, Smart-foto 16, Manfred Steinbach 7, Jan Martin Will 18; U.S. Navy 10; Wikipedia: 22

Publisher's note to educators and parents: Our editors have carefully reviewed the Web sites that appear on p. 31 to ensure that they are suitable for students. Many Web sites change frequently, however, and we cannot guarantee that a site's future contents will continue to meet our high standards of quality and educational value. Be advised that students should be closely supervised whenever they access the Internet.

Printed in the United States of America
1 2 3 4 5 6 7 8 9   12 11 10

CPSIA compliance information: Batch #BRW0102GS: For further information contact Gareth Stevens, New York, New York at 1-800-542-2595.

Contents

How Does a Helicopter Work?

Helicopters come in many different shapes and sizes, but they all share certain parts. These include a powerful engine and spinning rotor blades.

The rotor hub connects the rotor blades to the engine.

Gears transfer power from the engine to the rotor blades.

Hot gases leave the engine through the exhaust.

The pilot controls the helicopter from the cockpit.

The pilot uses two control columns to control the speed and direction of the helicopter.

The pilot uses foot pedals to turn the helicopter from side to side.

The Sea King rescue helicopter has wheels for landing gear.

The tailplane makes the helicopter stable.

The tail rotor balances the twisting force of the rotor blades to stop the helicopter from spinning around.

The rescue crew uses radar to navigate (find its way).

The tail rotor drive connects the engine to the tail rotor.

The rotor blades provide the lift force so the helicopter can fly.

The rescue crew and passengers sit in the cabin.

Rescue helicopters such as this Sea King have winches to lift people out of danger.

A "water wing" helps the helicopter to float if it has to land in the sea.

History of Helicopters

Helicopters are a modern invention that first appeared in the 1940s, but the idea for a helicopter had been around for hundreds of years before then.

Italian artist, engineer, and scientist Leonardo da Vinci (1452–1519) was the first person to think about a design for a helicopter. He made drawings of amazing flying machines in his notebook. One of the drawings was a machine that could fly straight up and down like a helicopter. Leonardo's design was well ahead of its time, but the materials did not then exist for his dream to become a reality.

This is a page of one of Leonardo da Vinci's notebooks, showing his early drawing of a helicopter-like flying machine.

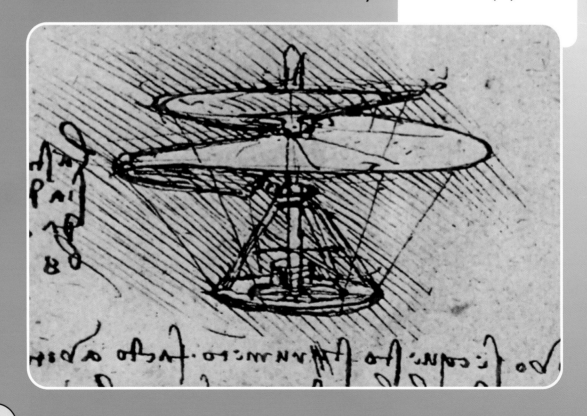

THAT'S AMAZING!

More than 1,500 years ago, the Chinese made kites that flew with wings that could spin around in the wind like the rotor blades of a helicopter.

All modern helicopters are based on Sikorsky's design.

Flying machines

American brothers Orville (1871–1948) and Wilbur Wright (1867–1912) designed and built the first airplane, called *Flyer,* in 1903. Four years later, engineers in France built a flying machine called the *Gyroplane.* It had four rotors and a small engine, but it only had enough power to fly a few feet off the ground.

In 1923, the autogyro was invented by Spanish engineer Juan de la Cierva (1895–1936). The autogyro had propellers at the front like an airplane, but the wings were replaced with four large rotors. These rotors spun around when the autogyro moved forward.

Modern helicopters

Russian-born American engineer Igor Sikorsky (1889–1972) invented the first helicopter in 1939. His VS-300 helicopter had a small gas-powered engine, a rotor with three main blades, and a tail rotor for stability.

Flying Forces

Helicopters fly in a similar way to airplanes. The spinning rotors create a lift force that pushes up on the rotor blades, lifting the helicopter off the ground.

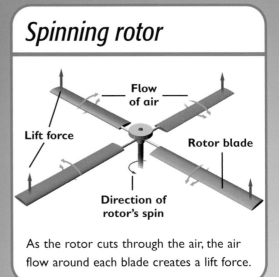

Spinning rotor

Flow of air

Lift force

Rotor blade

Direction of rotor's spin

As the rotor cuts through the air, the air flow around each blade creates a lift force.

Weight is the force of gravity pulling down on the helicopter. Thrust is the forward force generated by the engines. Drag is the rubbing force of the air on the helicopter, which slows it down. The helicopter will rise up off the ground when the lift force is greater than the weight of the helicopter.

There are four main forces acting on a helicopter in flight.

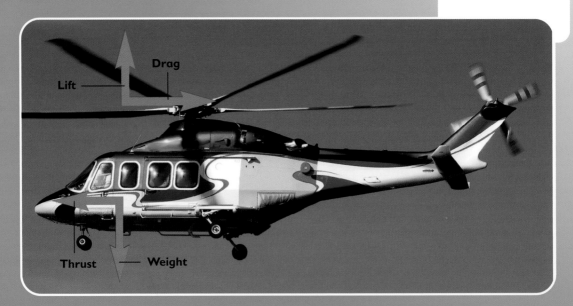

Drag

Lift

Thrust — Weight

Lift force

Each rotor blade is shaped like the wing of an airplane. When the pilot starts the engine, the rotors start to spin around. Air flows over each rotor blade. Air flows faster over the rotor blade than under it. This is because it has farther to move over the curved upper surface of the blade. Fast-moving air above the rotor blade has a lower pressure than the slow-moving air below the rotor blade. This difference in air pressure creates the lift force that pushes the helicopter up into the air.

TRY FOR YOURSELF

Create lift force

Try this experiment to see how the shape of a rotor blade creates lift force:

You will need:
• paper • sticky tape • ruler • hair dryer

1 Bend a piece of paper in half.

2 Tape the top half to the bottom half to make a curved top surface.

3 Hold the paper with a ruler. Blow the surface of the paper with a hair dryer.

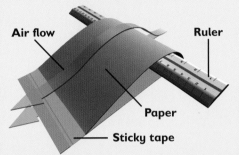

Air flow Ruler Paper Sticky tape

4 The paper lifts up when the air flows around it just like the rotor blade of a helicopter.

Lift action of a rotor blade

Twisting the rotor blade increases the angle of the blade. Air flowing over the rotor blade travels much faster than air flowing under the rotor blade. This creates a bigger lift force.

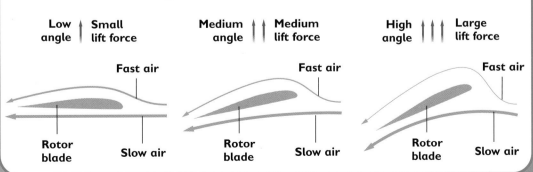

| Low angle | Small lift force | Medium angle | Medium lift force | High angle | Large lift force |

Fast air — Rotor blade — Slow air

In a Spin

The rotor is one of the most important parts of a helicopter. The pilot uses it to fly and steer the helicopter.

The rotor sits directly on top of the helicopter. The rotor hub connects the rotor blades to the engine. The engine powers the rotor drive, which moves the rotor hub. This makes the whole rotor spin around.

Drag hinges

The rotor blades come under a lot of forces as they spin around. Drag is the rubbing force of the air on the body of the helicopter.

The tail rotor

When the rotor spins around, it generates a force called torque. This would make the helicopter spin around the other way if it were not for the tail rotor to keep it steady. The pilot also uses the tail rotor to steer the helicopter.

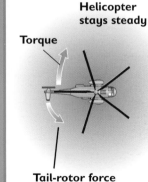

Helicopter stays steady

Torque

Tail-rotor force

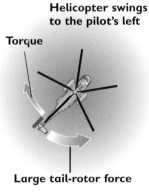

Helicopter swings to the pilot's left

Torque

Large tail-rotor force

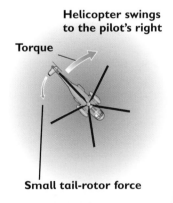

Helicopter swings to the pilot's right

Torque

Small tail-rotor force

A pilot inspects the rotor of his helicopter.

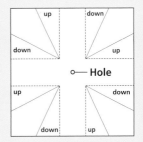
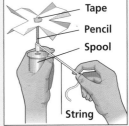
Drag also pushes against the blades as they spin through the air. The blades have drag hinges that can move in the air currents so the rotor blades do not snap.

Flapping hinges

The rotor blades would also break without flapping hinges. These hinges let the blades move up and down to lift the helicopter off the ground and steer it as it flies.

Pitch hinges

The pilot controls the pitch of the rotor blades to steer the helicopter. The pitch of the blade is the angle it makes with the ground. Pitch hinges let each rotor blade twist up and down.

Twisting and Turning

Helicopter pilots steer by changing the pitch and speed of the main rotor and tail rotor.

A helicopter pilot steers in two ways. To move up and down and hover in one spot, the pilot changes the pitch of all the rotor blades at the same time. This is called collective pitch control. Air flows faster over the top of each blade as the pitch increases. This increases the lifting force that pushes the helicopter up into the air.

A Merlin helicopter sweeps low over the ground.

Changing pitch to steer

The rotor blades have the same pitch. The helicopter rises straight up in the air.

The pitch of the rotor blades to the rear is greater than those at the front. The helicopter flies forward.

The pitch of the rotor blades on the right side is greater than those at the left. The helicopter flies sideways to the left.

Pitch controls

Collective pitch control changes the angle of the blades by the same amount so they all produce the same lift force.

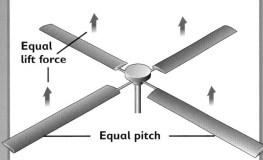

Equal lift force

Equal pitch

Cyclic pitch control changes the angle of each blade separately so the pilot can steer the helicopter.

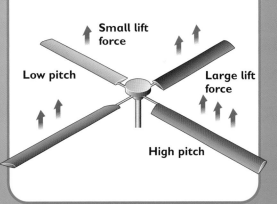

Small lift force

Low pitch

Large lift force

High pitch

The pilot can also change the pitch of each individual rotor blade. This creates different lift forces under different parts of the rotor blades. For example, the helicopter will tilt forward if the lift force is pushing up more at the back than the front of the rotor. This is because the rear rotor blades have a greater pitch than the front rotor blades, which pushes the helicopter forward. This is called cyclic pitch control.

Steering with the tail rotor

The pilot can also steer the helicopter with the tail rotor. As we saw on pages 10–11, the tail rotor balances the twisting force of the main rotor. As a result, the tail rotor also controls the direction in which the helicopter faces. This is known as the yaw. Pilots control the yaw using foot pedals in the cockpit.

Helicopter Power

The first helicopters used gasoline or diesel engines to drive the rotors. Modern helicopters use the power of jet engines.

Modern helicopters use a type of jet engine called a turboshaft. In most jet planes, the force of the hot exhaust gases pushing out of the engine produces the forward thrust. In a turboshaft, the hot exhaust gases drive the rotors through a driveshaft and gearbox.

Jet power

Air taken in through the front of the helicopter is drawn into the turboshaft engine. A compressor inside the engine squeezes the air. This makes the air very hot. A pump then sprays fuel into the hot air. The fuel burns to create a stream of hot exhaust gases.

This picture shows the fins in the turbine of a helicopter engine.

Spinning power

The stream of hot exhaust gases moves through the engine. They hit a turbine—a drum with fins. The gases flow through the turbine, making it spin. The turbine is connected to the driveshaft, so it spins quickly, too. A gearbox changes the spin of the driveshaft into the spin of the rotors. The exhaust gases leave the engine through the exhaust outlet.

Get in gear

Try this experiment to find out how a helicopter gearbox works.

You will need:
• potato • knife • 12 toothpicks • 2 nails • card

1 Ask an adult to cut two thick slices of potato.
2 Push six toothpicks into the edge of each potato slice. Space them out evenly. Carefully push a nail through the center of each potato slice. Fix one slice to a piece of card.
3 Hold the other potato slice by the nail and twist it close to the slice on the card. Watch it rotate.

The gearbox on a helicopter changes the direction of the engine's spin to make the rotor blades spin.

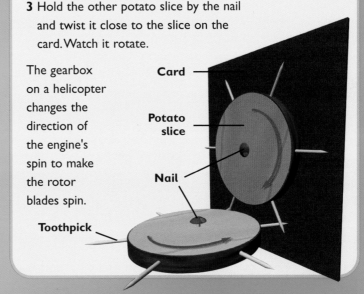

Card

Potato slice

Nail

Toothpick

Inside a helicopter engine

The turboshaft engine burns fuel in compressed air. This creates an explosion of hot exhaust gases that spins a turbine and drives a rotor.

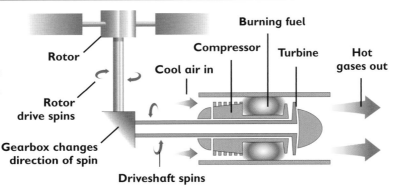

Rotor

Rotor drive spins

Gearbox changes direction of spin

Driveshaft spins

Burning fuel

Compressor

Cool air in

Turbine

Hot gases out

Taking Control

The controls in the cockpit allow the pilot and copilot to fly the helicopter. The cockpit includes a range of instruments that help the pilot and copilot to navigate and fly safely.

The cockpits of most helicopters have two seats—one for the pilot and one for the copilot. There are separate controls so both the pilot and copilot can fly the helicopter.

Fun Facts
Control systems are displayed on the inside of a helicopter pilot's helmet visor so that he or she can look at the controls and see where he or she is going at the same time.

Flight-information panel   Engine gauges   Engine controls   Radio equipment   Control column

The pilot steers the helicopter using the control columns.
Instruments in the cockpit tell the pilot what the helicopter is doing.

In control

The main helicopter controls are the yaw pedals, the throttle control, the collective-pitch control column, and the cyclic-pitch control column.

The collective-pitch control column moves up and down to move the helicopter up and down.

The pilot steers with the cyclic-pitch control column. This moves the helicopter forward, backward, and from side to side.

Pitch and speed

The yaw pedals control the pitch of the tail rotor. The pilot or copilot pushes the left yaw pedal to swing, or yaw, the helicopter to the left. The pilot or copilot pushes the right yaw pedal to yaw to the right.

The throttle handle is on the collective-pitch control column. The pilot or copilot twists the throttle handle to increase or decrease power from the engine.

A helicopter pilot prepares for takeoff.

Steering controls

The collective-pitch control column moves up and down to make the helicopter move up and down.

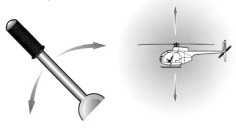

The cyclic control column controls the direction of the helicopter.

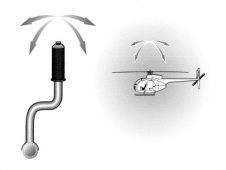

Landing Gear

Helicopters can take off and land just about anywhere. Different landing gear is needed for different surfaces.

Many helicopters have landing gear called skids, which are a bit like skis. Helicopters with skids can land on most surfaces, from hard concrete to soft mud.

Most large helicopters have wheels. They move under their own power, or they can be towed along by a tractor. Helicopters with wheels pull the landing gear inside

A helicopter flies across a remote glacier in Alaska. If you look closely at the landing gear you will see it has both skids and floats.

This picture shows the landing gear of a helicopter with wheels. The wheels can be pulled back up inside the helicopter when it is flying.

Landing gear

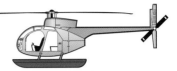

Helicopters with floats can land on almost any surface, including water.

Helicopters with skids can land on hard surfaces, such as concrete, and soft surfaces, such as snow.

Helicopters with wheels can only land on hard surfaces. They can also move along the ground.

the aircraft when they fly. This reduces drag and improves control. The pilot must take care when he or she releases the wheels before landing. Otherwise the helicopter can spin out of control and crash.

Landing on water

Search-and-rescue helicopters have "water wings." If the helicopter lands in the sea, the water wings inflate to help it float. The body of the helicopter is also shaped like a boat to help it float.

THAT'S AMAZING!

Some military ships carry helicopters. In heavy seas, the helicopter would fall off the deck if it wasn't for the strong locks that bolt the landing gear to the ship's surface.

Emergency Landings

When the engines fail and the rotor stops spinning, the pilot must know how to land safely using a technique called autorotation.

Helicopters cannot glide to land like an airplane. If the engines fail, the pilot can guide the helicopter to a safe landing by making the rotor spin around by itself. This is called autorotation.

Falling down

When the engine cuts out, the main rotor and tail rotor slow down. The helicopter turns sharply to one side as it loses thrust from the engine.

This helicopter has made an emergency landing in the snow.

TRY FOR YOURSELF

Make a rotor

Make your own rotor and watch it spin slowly to the ground.

You will need: • paper • pencil • ruler • scissors • paperclip

1 Copy the drawing shown here onto a piece of paper. Cut along the dotted lines to make two flaps.

2 Cut out the two long rectangles at the end and attach a paperclip to the remaining rectangle. Fold down the flaps.

3 Drop the rotor. See it spin slowly to the ground.

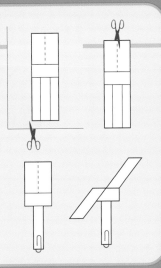

It begins to fall, nose first, toward the ground. As soon as this happens, the pilot keeps the nose straight using the yaw pedals. The pilot also flattens the rotors using the collective-pitch control column.

Safe landing

As the helicopter falls, air starts to flow up through the rotor blades. The rotor blades start to spin, creating a small lift force. The helicopter is autorotating. The pilot can then guide it to the ground. The helicopter is still falling very quickly. Just before the helicopter hits the ground, the pilot raises the nose by increasing the pitch of the rotor blades. This slows the helicopter enough to land it.

Autorotation landings

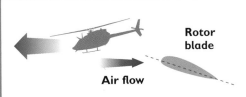

The air flows over the rotor blades from the front when the helicopter is flying normally.

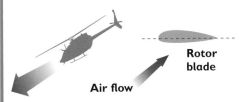

The air flows from underneath the rotor blades when the helicopter is falling in an emergency. This creates a lift force.

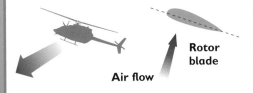

Increasing the pitch of the rotor blades slows the helicopter down and raises its nose to land safely.

Building Helicopters

All helicopters must be light but strong enough to cope with the extreme forces during flight. Different helicopters are built in different ways, depending on their use.

The earliest flying machines were wooden frames covered with stretched fabric. These structures were very weak and broke apart easily. When the first helicopters appeared in the 1940s, engineers used metal tubes, such as aluminum, and alloys to build them.

Building the body

The main body of the helicopter is called the fuselage. Small, lightweight helicopters used for crop spraying and other short journeys do not fly very quickly so they do not have to be very strong.

The Cornu helicopter was built in France in 1907. It was the first helicopter design to become airborne, but it only stayed in the air for less than a minute.

Large search-and-rescue helicopters need to be made of much stronger materials so they can withstand more extreme flying forces. All the working parts of a helicopter are usually made from metal because they need to be very strong.

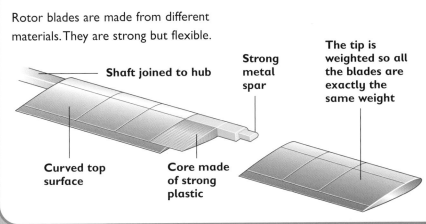

Rotor blades are made from different materials. They are strong but flexible.

Shaft joined to hub

Strong metal spar

The tip is weighted so all the blades are exactly the same weight

Curved top surface

Core made of strong plastic

helicopter strong but light, so it can fly much faster.

Size matters
Large helicopters are usually made from a framework of metal tubes. Metal panels stretch over the framework to form a "skin." Rivets hold the panels in place over the fuselage. This makes the

Small helicopters are often covered with a skin of lightweight materials such as plastic or fiberglass. These materials are cheap and easy to mold into shape. The panels are either glued or bolted onto the fuselage.

Fast Facts

- *Carbon fiber absorbs the vibration caused by the helicopter's engines. This stops the helicopter from ripping itself apart.*
- *Helicopters can have between two and eight blades depending on their use.*
- *Many plastics are now stronger than some metals. In the future, all helicopters may be built from these modern materials.*

Types of Helicopters

Helicopters come in many different shapes and sizes. Some have two or more rotors, while others lack the tail rotor typical of most other helicopters.

Helicopter design has changed very little since 1939, when Igor Sikorsky built the VS-300 helicopter. Most helicopters have one main rotor in the middle of the aircraft and one tail rotor at the rear.

Twin rotors

Some modern helicopters have more than one main rotor. They do not need a tail rotor to keep them stable. The rotors spin in opposite directions to cancel

THAT'S AMAZING!

Helicopters that fly to remote places, such as the desert or sea, have two engines. If one of the engines fails, the other takes over so the pilot can fly to safety.

Helicopter types

Single rotor helicopters (1) have tail rotors. Coaxial (2) and intermeshing (3) helicopters do not have tail rotors. Tandem (4) and quad (5) helicopters have multiple rotors to provide the lift force to carry heavy loads.

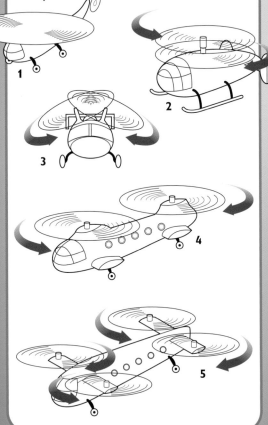

The Chinook is a tandem helicopter designed to carry troops and military equipment over long distances.

intermeshing helicopter has two main rotors. Some helicopters have two or more rotors. They are usually used to carry heavy loads. Tandem helicopters have two rotors—one above the cockpit and one above the engine in the tail. Quads have four rotors—two above the cockpit and two at the tail.

Convertiplanes

Convertiplanes are a cross between an airplane and a helicopter. When it is on the ground, its huge propellers point up. They work like helicopter rotors to lift the aircraft directly up into the air. The propellers point forward, and the machine flies like a normal airplane.

out the torque forces. One design is called the coaxial helicopter. It has two main rotors—one on top of the other. Coaxial helicopters do not have tail rotors. Instead, they have wide tailplanes to make them more stable. The

Helicopter to airplane

A convertiplane takes off like a helicopter. The propeller engines then turn to face forward. The convertiplane then flies like a normal airplane.

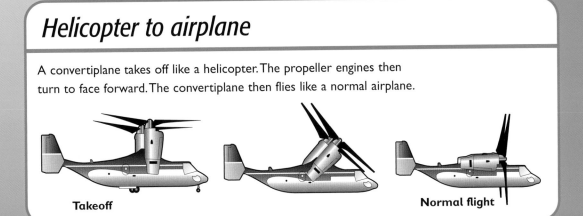

Takeoff

Normal flight

Helicopters at Work

Helicopters are highly maneuverable. They can get to places other aircraft cannot reach. This makes them useful in many different situations.

Helicopters have many uses. Military helicopters move troops and their equipment quickly. Helicopters are also used as air ambulances, for search-and-rescue missions, and even on farms for herding sheep and spraying crops.

Search and rescue

Search-and-rescue helicopters use radar (radio detection and ranging) to find people in danger. One crew member uses a radar machine to send beams of radio waves to search for people in distress. The machine listens for the echoes that

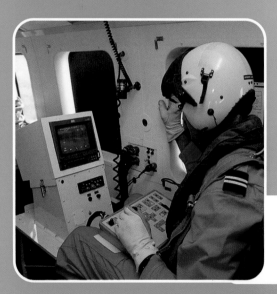

Pulled to safety

Helicopter winches can be used to lift a person directly out of danger or help them climb to safety.

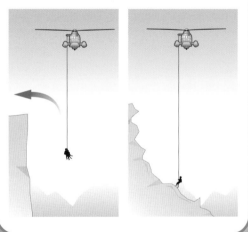

A crew member works the radar machine on a search-and-rescue mission.

A Coast Guard search-and-rescue team uses a winch to rescue a man drowning in the ocean.

happens in a remote place or when there is too much traffic for a normal ambulance to get to an accident in time. Air ambulances are very small, so they can land in small spaces on the road and between buildings. Hospitals usually have landing pads so the helicopters can land safely.

bounce off objects, such as sinking ships. Another crew member uses a winch to rescue people.

Air ambulance

Helicopters are used as ambulances when an emergency

THAT'S AMAZING!

Farmers who own large farms often use helicopters to herd livestock such as sheep and cattle. Since the herds are spread out over a wide area, they can be seen more easily from the air. Farmers also use helicopters to spray their land with fertilizers and pesticides.

Transporters

Helicopters are often used to carry people from place to place. Large helicopters carry workers to and from oil platforms at sea or to other remote places such as mountaintops. Other helicopters carry building materials to inaccessible places, such as the top of tall buildings.

Helicopters in the Future

No one knows what the helicopters of the future will look like. Engineers are developing helicopters that will travel faster and carry more passengers. Some helicopters may even break the sound barrier and one day fly into space.

The latest helicopters use jet engines and rockets to fly at high speed. One design is called the coaxial helicopter (see pages 24–25). These machines use two rotors— one on top of the other—to fly like an airplane when the engine power stops. The fixed rotors of the coaxial helicopter act like an X-shaped wing. The jet engines on each side of the coaxial helicopter can then be used to make the aircraft fly.

Rocket choppers

One new helicopter that engineers are designing may use the energy in the exhaust gases to turn the rotor blades. The engine directs the gases to flow out of the tips of the rotor blades, so each blade acts like a miniature rocket.

The Roton has propellers at the top of its dome-like shape. It lands on four feet at its base.

One advantage of tip-driven rotor blades is that the helicopter does not need a tail rotor. This is because the turning force of the rotor comes directly from the rotor itself—not the body of the helicopter.

Helicopters in space

Space scientists are developing spacecraft that use a helicopter-like machine that will force fuel through a rocket engine. The spacecraft could fly into space using the rotor-powered rocket, but fall back down to Earth under the force of the spinning blades. One day, this system may be able to launch satellites and astronauts into space.

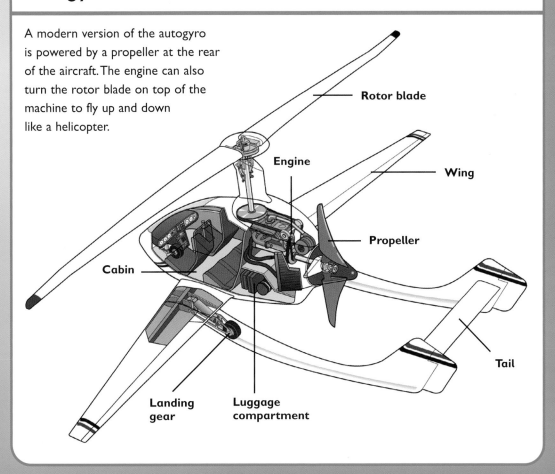

Autogyro

A modern version of the autogyro is powered by a propeller at the rear of the aircraft. The engine can also turn the rotor blade on top of the machine to fly up and down like a helicopter.

Rotor blade

Engine

Wing

Propeller

Cabin

Landing gear

Luggage compartment

Tail

Glossary

autorotation: when a rotor spins around on its own to create lift

collective pitch: a control that changes the pitch of all the rotor blades by the same amount

control column: like the steering wheel of an automobile, the pilot uses the control column to steer the helicopter

convertiplanes: aircraft that are a cross between an airplane and a helicopter

cyclic pitch: a control that changes the pitch of each rotor blade by a different amount

drag: the rubbing force of the air on the body of the helicopter that slows it down

engine: part of a helicopter that provides the power to move it forward

exhaust: the waste gases released from an engine after it has burned the fuel

fiberglass: a type of plastic made up of many fine glasslike threads

force: a push or pull on an object

fuselage: the main body of a helicopter

gears: the parts that help to control the speed of the engine and the direction of rotation

gravity: the force of attraction between different masses

hover: to stay in the same place in midair

lift: the upward force created by the difference in air pressure above and below the helicopter's rotor blades

navigation: finding your way

pitch: the angle of the rotor blade

pressure: the amount of force acting on a surface

propeller: a metal disk with blades that spins around to push an aircraft through the air

radar: short for radio detection and ranging, radar finds objects by bouncing radio waves off them

rotor blade: a long, thin, curved winglike object in the rotor of a helicopter

satellite: an object that orbits Earth. Pilots use satellites to help them find their way.

skids: one type of landing gear on a helicopter. Skids look a little bit like skis. They allow helicopters to land on most surfaces, from hard concrete to soft snow.

speed: the distance traveled in a given time

throttle: part of a helicopter that controls the power of the engine

thrust: the forward force generated by the engine of a helicopter

torque: a force that makes an object spin around

turbine: a set of blades in a drum that spin when driven by the exhaust gases of a jet engine

turboshaft: a type of jet engine used to power a helicopter

weight: the force of gravity pushing down on a helicopter

winch: a simple machine used to lift and lower objects on the end of a strong rope or cable

yaw: the circular side-to-side movement of a helicopter

Further Information

Books to read:

Beck, Paul. *Flight Test Lab: Helicopters*. Berkeley, CA: Silver Dolphin Books, 2004.

Goodman, Susan E. *Choppers!* New York: Random House, 2004.

Web sites to look at:

www.explainthatstuff.com/helicopter.html

www.howstuffworks.com/helicopter.htm

Museums to visit:

American Helicopter Museum & Education Center, West Chester, Pennsylvannia. www.helicoptermuseum.org

National Helicopter Museum, Stratford, Connecticut. www.nationalhelicoptermuseum.org

Index